AM I RUNNING WITH YOU, GOD?

Other Books by Malcolm Boyd

CRISIS IN COMMUNICATION

CHRIST AND CELEBRITY GODS

FOCUS

IF I GO DOWN TO HELL

THE HUNGER, THE THIRST

ARE YOU RUNNING WITH ME, JESUS?

FREE TO LIVE, FREE TO DIE

MALCOLM BOYD'S BOOK OF DAYS

THE FANTASY WORLDS OF PETER STONE
AND OTHER FABLES

AS I LIVE AND BREATHE:
STAGES OF AN AUTOBIOGRAPHY

MY FELLOW AMERICANS

HUMAN LIKE ME, JESUS

THE LOVER

WHEN IN THE COURSE OF HUMAN EVENTS
(WITH PAUL CONRAD)

THE RUNNER

THE ALLELUIA AFFAIR

CHRISTIAN

Am I Running With You, God?
Malcolm Boyd

DOUBLEDAY & COMPANY, INC.
GARDEN CITY, NEW YORK
1977

The author and publisher express their appreciation to the following for permission to include the material indicated:

Abba, a Journal of Prayer for pages 10 and 12, which appeared in volume 1, number 1 (Easter, 1976) as "God is here, right now."

The Christian Century for pages 48, 50, 52, 54, 56, 58, 60, 62, 64, 66, 88, 102, 104, and 136. Copyright © 1975 by the Christian Century Foundation. Reprinted by permission.

Christian Herald for pages 49, 51, 53, 55, 57, 59, 61, 63, 65, and 67, which appeared as "Meditations in Jerusalem" (March 4, 1975). Copyright © 1975 by the Christian Herald Association. Reprinted by permission.

The New York Times for page 122, which appeared in the May 30, 1976, issue, Op-Ed page, as "Thou Shalt Not Stump in the Pulpit." Copyright © 1976 by The New York Times Company. Reprinted by permission.

Selected scripture passages are from
the Authorized Version, the Revised Standard Version,
and the New English Bible.

ISBN: 0-385-12364-7
Library of Congress Catalog Card Number 76–50793
Copyright © 1975, 1977 by MALCOLM BOYD
ALL RIGHTS RESERVED
PRINTED IN THE UNITED STATES OF AMERICA
First Edition

To
*Those who have learned integrity and dignity
in their lives . . .
look into the Lord's face and laugh
with grateful joy.*

CONTENTS

Chapter I

Ecstasy

I have swum in a lake past a gaunt, windswept pine tree that cast a moving shadow on the water, and felt that I knew how a Druid might have thought about finding a sign of holiness in such a scene. I have stood in the vast sand reaches of the Sinai and looked up at towering peaks thrust into the sky, and felt that I knew how an ancient nomad thought about finding a sense of the mysterium tremendum there. I have felt profound awe of God as I stood next to the darkening waters of a Greek sea at dusk; atop Mount Zion when the sun cast the first ray of light into the morning sky; inside a great cathedral as I walked on tiles that were worn by the feet of pilgrims through past centuries; in the heart of a city at 3 a.m., when its fury was leashed by sleep and its people dreamed dreams.

I am as conscious of experiencing God everywhere in life as a medieval person residing in the shadow of Chartres or an ancient tribal person living close to the realities of nature.

In my view, God is quite beyond a definition or limitation. God is not created in my, or anyone else's, image. God does not "exist" because of my, or anyone else's, need. God's spirit can dance with happiness as well as pent-up rage; cry out in anguish and ecstasy; mourn and celebrate.

God is here with me, right now.

I LONG FOR THE RUNNING OF THIS NEW DAY

The sky lightens. You are changing the stage lights for the next act, God. It is a silent, hushed, quiet scene.

Here comes the new day with all its possibilities. It excites me, filling me with joy and wonder. My thoughts race ahead to the new decisions that you will soon show me in the quickly coming day.

Yesterday my pride was dealt an unexpected and cruel blow. I reacted instinctively by retreating far within myself, trying to block and cut off feeling. I felt that I could not face the world again. I coudl not bear to look into its mocking eyes.

Your eyes, Lord, do not mock me. Thank you for healing me with love.

The running of the new day has begun. I pray you, Lord, let me be fulfilled in your will.

Am I running with you, God? Let it be so. Let it be so, Lord.

When I have run away from God and hidden in order to avoid entanglement and involvement, God has pursued me. When I assumed an overly indulgent relation with God that I felt approached being chummy, God awed me with sternness and majesty, remainding me of the reality of judgment. "O my soul, be prepared for the coming of the Stranger, Be prepared for him who knows how to ask questions," T. S. Eliot wrote. When I made an assumption that God had grown distant from me in majesty, God suddenly appeared as one who cares intensely and passionately for the most minute act of human justice, mercy, and love.

If I tried to explain God in utterly simplistic terms, God came to me as a Trinity. If I became dazzled and confused by God's intricacy and complexity, God spoke directly to my heart and reminded me to become childlike.

I experience God in labyrinth, by quicksand, in tumult and silence.

And in stable, ordinary things. So I visit an ancient tree whose majesty, awesome friendliness, and sheer beauty take one's breath away. The tree is a close friend of mine. I touch its body lovingly, commune with it as I sit beneath a mass of leaves or ice-covered boughs, ponder its mystery and my own, and marvel at this companion who will outlive me on the earth.

THE MYSTERY OF CREATION
IS IN MY OWN BEING, GOD

Inside my body, mind, and soul can be found the towering peak of an unfound mountain, the unwalled city of an ocean floor, a quiet river sanctuary, and a vast desert whose raging storms scare immense birds.

Despite the glory and assurance of your creation, God, I have perplexing questions to ask you.

Can I know if I have gained the world?

Can I know if I have lost my soul?

O Lord, speak to me in the labyrinth, by the quicksand, in the tumult, and in the silence. Tell me, God. Instruct me. Penetrate my heart. Change me, God, so that your ways will be my ways. Overwhelm my stubborn pride. Make me yours.

How does one define God?

Surely an ultimate absurdity is a picture of a dozen people seated around a table engaged in meticulously composing the compleat definition of God—as well as articles of heresy directed at those who disagree.

Anne Hutchinson comes to mind as a real victim of such absurdity. Mistress Hutchinson was banished to Rhode Island in 1637 because of her claim that she received "direct revelation from God." This marked her as "different" and tended to equate her with the nonconformist Quakers, who were called outsiders.

That happened more than three hundred years ago. Yet tolerance as an act of compassion based on belief in God is even now sometimes found to be lacking.

A deeply ingrained macho image of God is, I suspect, a result of a male-engendered campaign to "create" God in a supermasculine image, one to be manipulated in order to maintain societal power. There is a female semblance of God as well as a masculine one. But God transcends anthropomorphism. As much as God chooses to be revealed in our lives, nonetheless there are hidden aspects of God. This reality is so threatening to many people that they refuse to acknowledge its existence.

SIX LINES

There are six lines in the sky. The time is near sunset. I find my-self in an airplane, ready to land at an airport.

The lines are jet streaks made by six other planes that have apparently just taken off, within minutes of one another.

Looking at these lines, drawn as if by a pencil in the blue and red sky that holds the hot afternoon sun in its orbit, my thoughts turn momentarily to wonderment. The wild beauty of the sky, and the incredible precision of the six lines that never meet even as they are still being drawn upon its body, abruptly stun my senses.

Now I reach out to you in my senses, the direction of my thoughts, the thrust of my being, God. The mystery of life and death, creation and such bewildering wonder in the cosmos, over-whelm my knowing and imagination. How can I bear its longing and intensity?

God, are you austere or sensuous, long-suffering or quick to anger? Are you knowable to me?

God, how may I perceive what you want me to do?

God is the single great thread running through the entirety of my life. When I have seemed to break this thread of relationship, God has mended it.

As a child I did not worry about who God was. Essentially God seemed to be comforting, a stable and wholesome base in the midst of complexity. There was the awareness of Someone to whom was addressed a nightly prayer. "Now I lay me down to sleep." The Someone was God. "If I die before I wake." I believed that I would be safe. "Pray the Lord my soul to take." Wasn't God my friend? Surely such a friend would not inflict hurt.

I never doubted that God was my confidant as I struggled to survive.

When I was seven years old I wrote a prayer. This is it:

> Your Holy father is in your temple
> a temple is when your good pray
> and thank your Holy father
> for what He is doing all the time
> for you your Holy father gives
> you the world and a Home clothes
> water air Food you should thank
> him for it at least five times a
> day everybody should love there
> Holy father God: AMEN.

I HAVE TO ASK SOMETIMES:
IS HELL ON THIS EARTH?

I know so many tormented people, God. It seems that hell burns in the interior of many haunted and despairing souls.

Yet I, too, know this experience. In this awful moment I must ask you: Where has my faith gone? I feel drained, barren, listless. I can scarcely gather the necessary strength to pick up a pencil or walk outside the door, smile at another person or exchange a human greeting.

I despise my very motives. I cannot forgive my actions, God. But I refuse to turn to you for forgiveness or the blessing of a fresh beginning.

So, I am trapped in a tight vise of my own construction. I can turn neither to the left nor to the right.

Why do you stay with me when I shout at you to go away and leave me alone in these conflicts and agonies? But you continue to love me even as I am unlovable.

What can I say to you in this moment when I know that I have been delivered out of a hell in which I so bitterly and unhappily existed? Anguish is a harrowing experience. I am deeply grateful for your love. I can, and do, say thank you, God.

I can still remember when a youthful friend of mine, a class-mate in school, died unexpectedly. Young death of this kind is inexpressibly sorrowful and perplexing. It represents a life that didn't have a chance to get started here. It occurred to me that God, my friend who the church said was omnipotent, omniscient, and omnipresent, should have been able to prevent this youthful death.

Frankly, I was confused. There was the slightest glimmering in my mind that God may not have wanted to spare my young friend's life. But in that case, wasn't God acting evilly? I said to myself: After all, who cared what God, with all of his arbitrary power, wanted? Wasn't God supposed to be simply loving? Didn't God, just because of being God, have to be loving?

But what I was really doing was demanding that God perform according to my dictate and wishes, and enact love simplistically in accord with my own definition of it. I wanted to determine how my prayers would be answered.

YOU ARE PUSHING ME, GOD

Spring is here. It tells me that you are impelling me to move forward once again into a new dimension of being. This past winter was hard. I remember unyielding ice when death visited my house. It left a scar inside me that is unhealed, demanding, and immediate.

Forgive me, but even if I could give up my pain, I would not willingly do so at this time. It is my close link to someone loved who has gone. Yet I know when spring turns to summer that I will be warmed by a returning sun. I will begin to forget. The pain will ebb.

This change, which I resist fiercely with a stubborn part of myself, will be thrust upon me and finally have its way. Despite my present façade of opposition, I offer thanks. For life beckons.

All my senses, my intellect, and my soul speak to me, telling me to smile at this change as a friend. God, I shall try. Meanwhile, spring is here. To my amazement, a pine tree seems to have grown a bit more in the past day. The universe is freshly green, except for the roses, azaleas, flags, and tulips that fill the garden. How can I not respond to this delight of your season, your providence?

Struggle with me, God. Have your way of peace, my Lord.

As I grew up, I discovered that it was absurd to "address" God formally. I felt God's intimate presence in my life. Yet I had been taught to perceive God in "the heavens," the mysterious and infinite star-filled sky that radiated bright light out of the unfathomable depths of an unreachable dark void.

Somehow I knew that God was not really confined to being out there but was also very close. When I went away to college, I did not feel God's presence acutely anymore. Afterward formalism replaced intimacy with God again. About ten years ago I learned anew that there is warmth and love in God. Jesus isn't just back there on a cross, in a tomb, and ascending into the heavens; Jesus is here. Jesus sweats and laughs, works and cries, loves and hopes in this modern world. He is to be found in the midst of life.

I SIT AT A COFFEE COUNTER

Twenty or more people are seated here, drinking a cup of coffee, waiting for a refill, daydreaming, thinking about the future, reading a letter or the newspaper, and making plans for the day's work.

Jesus sits somewhere in this group.

Elsewhere among the people is a woman who works to support two sons. They're at a day-care center while she goes out to do her job.

A man in this group has lost his job this morning. He'll have another cup of coffee before calling his wife to tell her.

Another man here will be told by a doctor in a half hour whether he must make plans to undergo surgery.

A woman seated two places from him will meet a man this noon whom she will marry.

Jesus finishes his cup of coffee and walks out on the street.

Am I praying with you, Jesus?

In the past ten years hundreds of people have written letters to me, pouring out their feelings and asking questions. Many of these letters concern God.

"What I wanted to ask you, if it's not too personal, is how you became tired of being away from God, as I am," an American G.I. wrote.

A poignant letter was written by a woman who said: "I love God, but I don't know how to communicate with him. Maybe it's because I feel so unimportant. How do you reach out to other people? The world is so cold, and you get put back in your place so very quickly. For twenty years I repressed my emotions because I had been hurt as a child. Now I feel in order to be a whole person I must become outgoing and give a part of myself, no matter what. Life is so short. I am not too good with words or reaching out. Please understand. I simply need to know how to communicate with God."

I believe that the "how" of communication with God must inevitably involve a responsiveness from our human standpoint, an openness, even a simple vulnerability. Such responsiveness also needs to take solid form between ourselves and other people, for it is uniquely here that one encounters God.

I have felt the greatest love of God when I was with people. I have encountered God again and again in people.

THEY'RE PROPHETS, LORD, AND THEY'RE GAY

They stand inside your church, and know a wholeness that can benefit it. Long ago they learned that they must regard the lilies of the field, putting their trust in you.

Pressured to hide their identities and gifts, they have served you with an unyielding, fierce love inside the same church that condemned them.

Taught that they must feel self-loathing, nevertheless they learned integrity and dignity, and how to look into your face and laugh with grateful joy, Lord.

Victims of a long and continuing torture, they asserted a stubborn faith in the justice of your kingdom.

Negativism was drummed into them as thoroughly as if they were sheet metal. They learned what it is to be hated. Yet, despite such rejection, they insisted on attesting to the fullness and beauty of all human creation, including theirs, in your image.

They are alive and well and standing inside your church. Bless them, Lord, to your service.

In a moment of weakness and doubt, I virtually convinced myself that God and I should both be phony in our mutual relationship. This would mean locking ourselves into scripted roles that must always be undeviating. Fortunately, I discovered that God did not want to pull the strings of my, or anyone else's, life or treat us as if we were marionettes. God wanted me to be my own self, a growing one. God truly accepted me as someone involved in the continuing growth of becoming a more complete person. I was grateful.

I thanked God that God was God, not a capricious, ruthless, or self-centered deity lacking wholeness and truth.

I continue to thank God for this.

WHAT JUDGMENTS DO YOU MAKE, GOD?

It seems to me that you damn war, hate, hypocrisy, lies, tyranny, apartheid, torture, exploitation, and murder.

It seems to me that you bless love, peace, honesty, truth, freedom, co-operation, kindness, dignity that is rooted in your creation, and life.

I find that you work patiently and mercifully to change the things that you damn into what you bless.

Help me to keep faith with you, God.

I AM MALCOLM

This is my baptismal name.

I am male and a Christian.

I am an American and white.

And I am gay, as you know, Lord.

Essentially I am a person created in your image, God. I am also a sojourner, a pilgrim, a runner, and one who wishes to be free but still belong to a community.

I never liked masks, yet have felt forced at times to wear them. I have lived in two different parts of life, seemingly split down the middle of my being. Let my naked face now be seen by others as it is seen by you, Lord. Let me look upon the naked faces of others in all their created and natural beauty, and not upon fabricated, complex, painted masks that obscure truth.

Let me move closer into wholeness, and help others to do the same, as I openly share the fullness of my being. Why should any part of my life be withheld from communication with others or treated in a secret or shadowy way? For I am warmly and happily grateful for joy and love, and the unfettered sharing of these in your wondrous world.

I thank you with all my heart for my creation and wholeness, God.

Chapter II

Stillness

The stillness in which I found myself seemed to be pure. Certainly, I reasoned, it is safe. So I relaxed and felt at ease.

Abruptly I was under a deadly attack. I had not realized that the silence was filled by demons.

Soon I came under savage temptation. I was offered power if I would sell my soul in order to possess it. Glory and riches would be mine if I sacrificed my integrity and conscience.

I was offered unfettered dominion over the flesh if I would accept its yoke and tyranny, live solely in my body, and renounce love in favor of exploiting people.

Afterward I was tempted by a galaxy of spiritual prerogatives if I would renounce God for gods and consent to manipulate people's lives in such a way as to enslave their spirituality.

I fell on my knees in fear and desperation.

SERENITY IS YOUR BLESSING, GOD

Demons used to plague my life. I was deathly afraid of them. You taught me that I must name them, Lord, calling each one by its own name.

Anxiety gave me no peace.

Loneliness tortured me cruelly. I did not yet know the saving grace of solitude, that can banish loneliness by transforming it.

Insecurity instilled a restlessness in me that was finally banished only by the stable grace of gratitude for my deep security in you.

Pride laid siege to my life. It insinuated itself into every part of my being and doing. It exhorted me to see each friend as an enemy. It painted each potentially good encounter in my life as yet another threat to itself.

Thank you for teaching me how to come to know these demons intimately in moments of faith and stillness, calling them all by name. Now they are no longer unknown powers holding sway over me, causing terror and unhappiness in my life. Thank you for my freedom, Lord.

In faith, my mind reaches out to God in thoughts and words. In hope, my soul plays upon the harp and sings to God. In love, my body exults in jubilation in God's presence.

I beseech God to give me three things:

A sense of awe that will always penetrate my senses in love's presence.

A vulnerability to joy in love's presence.

An awareness of innocence in love's presence that will never leave me.

TENDERNESS TOUCHES ME GENTLY, GOD

I am moved by highly romantic and sentimental feelings. I play handball with the sun, tennis with the moon, and gamble recklessly with the stars between my fingers. It is fun to play in your world, with your world, God.

This moment of supreme happiness flees as if driven. In another moment it will be gone. But, Lord, you hold all the moments.

I cannot be sad that a moment dies when you, God, will still be with me in the next one.

In utter isolation I cried out as a stranger upon the face of the earth.

I thirsted for feeling and love.

I hungered to hold life in my hands, my arms, my mouth, and the fullness of my eyes.

I yearned for a sense of true relationship. I wanted to receive and give human respect and love.

Relationship was never so simple for me as rolling over like a log and falling into a nice fire. Invariably I wondered what were the human motivations and feelings of another person in my life.

It was all such a mystery to me—my existence, another person's existence, the fact that we knew each other; and the wonder that we had somehow managed to cut our way through endless complexity in order to find in present stillness the core of communication and joy.

MALCOLM BOYD

I REACH OUT AND TOUCH A TREE

It is your creation, Lord, as I am. I murmur something to the tree as I stroke it and show my love. I wonder if the tree, in its way, murmurs a word to me?

I experience calmness, tranquility, and restoration in this moment, God.

The universe is in a red bird that sits on a bough and looks at me. The universe is in me, too. The red bird and I regard the universe in each other. I feel kinship, warmth, and a sense of belonging to you, God.

I yearn for you, calling you to me. Yet even my call belongs to you and has its origin in you, Lord.

Once I wandered for a time sadly and aimlessly in a still laby-rinth of depression. I could not find my way out of endless corri-dors in my life that led nowhere.

I believed that I wanted to die, but had no clear idea what that meant.

Utmost fear and anxiety possessed me. I pursued twisted paths and sharp turns. A sign inside the corridors of my life announced: No Exit.

I AM AT REST

Just a short while ago I felt that I could neither breathe nor bear my heavy pain, God. A bitter, agonizing loneliness swept over me without warning. I wept in utter dread and panic.

I asked myself if one is ever absolutely alone and cut off from the presence of God. At that moment of anxiety I could see no hope or glimmering of light. I was lost and bereft in an alien, threatening, and totally inhospitable world.

But you put your hand on me, God. You let me know that you share all the pain with me. Now the pain has left me, and I feel sharp joy.

I bless and thank you, God. I am glad that your hand is on me.

One day I basked in what I supposed to be a warm glow of friendship. Without any warning it froze suddenly, becoming a core of ice.

Eyes that had laughed easily in intimate conversation with me changed into signals that were tense and angry. These offered me no sign of hope. Caring vanished. Betrayal was complete.

Every dream of kindness and goodness that I had ever nurtured seemed to become a sad illusion.

The universe had changed into a monstrous and cruel jungle of destruction and hatred.

THE WHOLE WORLD SEEMS TO BE MOTIONLESS

Is this so because I am, Lord?

I sit in darkness beneath an ancient tree waiting the coming of the light of day. Dawn is close by.

The mystery and goodness of the dark envelop me. My eyes of faith can see more clearly in the dark than my natural eyes can see in the light. I used to feel threatened by imaginary dangers and shadowy forms in the darkness, but now I find comfort and peace.

The darkness all about me is the sea, God. I play the part of a peaceful submarine. I lie quietly here on the sea floor. Now my engines are silent. I sleep. Fish swim around me, knowing I am their friend. We share the ocean floor, its beauty and goodness, in perfect peace.

Does your inner light burn steady in me, God?

Tumult came into my life in a rush of confusion, when true values were no longer visible to me.

The focus with which I was ordinarily accustomed to viewing the perspective of my life blurred.

The center of quiet and sanity inside my consciousness was battered incessantly by the tumult.

Yet the center held fast. God spoke to me there. He reasoned with me. The center spread out, taking hold of my life.

The tumult, as a storm, moved away.

STILLNESS IS SO MANY THINGS, LORD

In it one may hear the ticking of a clock, wind in trees, whispers, footsteps, and the great roar of the sea inside a seashell.

If there is enough stillness, and words are absent, one may hear the beat of another heart.

In a silence that speaks volumes, one hears unspoken words.

Outward silence may be accompanied by inner fury and a plethora of sound. Outward fury and sound may be accompanied by inner stillness.

You speak in stillness, God.

Oh let the fury of the world diminish, Lord. Let us wait upon you with still voices and hearts.

I placed faith in cerebral systems and neat logic. But then I found myself supping pleasantly in a most relaxed ambience while I watched bloody wars on color television.

Soon I became obsessed by the need of an explanation of the world's behavior and my own. This eluded me. So I gave myself up to energy and force. Could this save me from my experience of isolation in an ordered space of life? If not, perhaps it would at least afford an escape into the play of dancing shadows, the beat of drums, and a pulsating flow of memory and desire.

Yet there was neither salvation nor escape.

I was propelled by an obsessive need to discover, and confront, the meaning of life itself. Ultimately a vaulting, overarching need of transcendence stirred me to move resolutely outside the plastic shell in which I had existed.

DO DISTANT BELLS RING OUT
IN THE STILL MORNING AIR?

The earth is fresh. I feel at peace, God.

Life today resembles a vast, peaceful, fruitful land that I can see clearly from a green hill. Friendly white clouds that playfully resemble monsters hang in the sunny sky, casting shadows on the ground that become oases for travelers. Distant vistas and faraway lands are in my vision.

I want to sing at the top of my lungs. I need to shake and run, Lord, exulting and dancing with wild joy, running, running, running to you.

MY HANDS TOUCH, GRASP, AND MOVE

My legs stretch out, cross, walk, stand still, and run
My mouth tastes, eats, drinks, kisses, shouts, whispers, talks,
 closes, and opens
My stomach fills, empties, growls, hisses, and is silent
My shoulders bend, twist, lean over, and are straight
My hair is handsome, ugly, long, short, wavy, dry, oily,
 and falls out
My genitals are quiet, aroused, normal, mysterious, functional,
 private, and public
My back is unbending, bent, and filled with nerve ends
My head is the most familiar view of me held by most people
My heart is unseen as it pumps away, yet the character of it is
 seen by everybody in my actions all of the time
My eyes are the windows of my soul, although sometimes I try to
 pull down the shades
My body is a mystery, God. And so is my soul
Help me to understand their wholeness
I am grateful for my body, God
I want to give it food, drink, iron, tenderness, and love
I am grateful for my soul, God
I want to give it flowers, iron, humor, visions, and love
Thank you for sanctifying my life with the gift of wholeness.

Chapter III

Shalom

I found myself engaged in intense, often passionate conversations in Jerusalem during the winter of 1974–75. I lived for nearly three months as a guest of Mishkenot Sha'ananim, a retreat for the creative, whose windows look out at Mount Zion. A special project of Jerusalem's Mayor Teddy Kollek, it was dedicated on August 13, 1973, when Pablo Casals performed at a ceremony held in its gardens.

Mishkenot Sha'ananim has an enchanting history. In 1875 it was founded as the first Jewish settlement outside the walls of the Old City. Its origin was made possible by the endeavors of Sir Moses Montefiore of England and Judah Touro and Gersham Kursheedt of America. Mishkenot derives its name from Isaiah 32:18: "My people will abide in a peaceful habitation, in secure dwellings, and in quiet resting places."

My life at Mishkenot fell rapidly into a certain pattern. After an early breakfast I worked during the mornings in my apartment. Then I went for my long walks—up the Mount of Olives, around the Old City walls, sometimes with the Western ("Wailing") Wall or the Dome of the Rock, Absalom's Pillar, or the Lion's Gate as a focal point. My feet learned the contours of the city's paths and roads. In place of lunch I substituted a glass of fresh fruit juice or a bowl of steaming hot soup found along my way. In the afternoons I worked alone once again or else had an appointment with a painter, a writer, an editor, a professor, or a journalist. I interviewed dozens of Arabs and Jews. My evenings were filled by invitations to Jerusalem homes.

KING DAVID STILL DOMINATES JERUSALEM

Matthew's Gospel speaks of David's centrality: "There were thus fourteen generations in all from Abraham to David, fourteen from David until the deportation to Babylon, and fourteen from the deportation until the Messiah."

I stand inside King David's tomb atop Mount Zion.

Candles burn in front of the tomb, which is covered by a shroudlike robe. The tomb is inside a cave.

Now an elderly woman who wears a shawl over her head approaches the tomb. She kisses it. She mumbles prayers and cries out in her emotion. Her outpouring of faith and devotion continues for several moments. She makes entreaties to God.

When she departs, silence once again engulfs the interior of the cave. But soon a young woman enters accompanied by two small children. They pray aloud and light candles.

"The Lord loves the gates of Zion more than all the dwellings of Jacob; her foundations are laid upon holy hills, and he has made her his home."

One thing I loved in Israel was living by a Jewish clock. In December I went to see, not Handel's The Messiah, but Handel's Judas Maccabeus. Lovely. A fresh experience. On Friday afternoon the curtain of the Shabbat falls on the Jerusalem stage, not to be raised until Saturday evening. I read the International Herald Tribune and the Jerusalem Post, listened to the Voice of America, waited impatiently for the mail (it is very slow) to arrive in Jerusalem as well as reach the United States. I came to the realization that I was in a developing country, agonizingly watched prices in markets, and shared a sense of danger from terrorists' grenades, even as I knew that I was safer on a Jerusalem street than an equivalent one in New York, Chicago, or San Francisco. I went to dance and symphony concerts, visited coffeehouses and the cinema, and enjoyed reading the works of Israeli authors before I met them.

Jerusalem, the Holy City, has many moods. Sometimes it is modern with radios blaring music and cars speeding by. At other times it withdraws into the ancient recesses of its past, its face veiled or inscrutable.

I have climbed to the city's hills, wandered along its paths and streets, talked and listened to its people, and known its moods.

But especially I have visited its places of particular religious meaning. There I have thought deeply, meditated, and prayed.

THE UPPER ROOM IS ABSOLUTELY STILL

I try to move back through the centuries, through dogmas and religious controversies and wars. Does Jesus stand in the center of this upstairs room with its ancient windows and cracked stone floor?

"During supper he took bread, and having said the blessing he broke it and gave it to them, with the words: 'Take this; this is my body.' Then he took a cup, and having offered thanks to God he gave it to them; and they all drank from it. And he said, 'This is my blood of the covenant, shed for many. I tell you this: never again shall I drink from the fruit of the vine until the day when I drink it new in the kingdom of God.'"

There is an extraordinary sense of sharing Jesus' presence within this room. Light coming through the windows falls in a simple pattern on the stone floor. Cobwebs stretch across the windows.

Now voices come up from below. A man speaks. A woman responds. Children shout. It has become a clamor.

"Then they returned to Jerusalem from the hill called Olivet, which is near Jerusalem, no farther than a Sabbath day's journey. Entering the city they went to the room upstairs. . . . Suddenly there came from the sky a noise like that of a strong driving wind. . . . And there appeared to them tongues like flames of fire. . . . And they were all filled with the Holy Spirit and began to talk in other tongues, as the Spirit gave them power of utterance."

The voice of humanity itself beats persistently against the constant shore of this Upper Room where the dynamic of religious faith was set in motion for all time.

Israel formally joins the state with religion, yet many of its people separate the practice of organized religion from their lives. Israelis, however, raise religious questions. A thirty-five-year-old French-born woman, an immigrant five years earlier, told me that when she came to Israel she had nothing to do with religion at all. Last year she began to light candles on Friday nights and to make at least a partial observance of the Shabbat. She goes to the Western Wall only on special occasions three or four times a year and is always spiritually shaken—deeply so—when she goes there. She has never visited Yad Vashem, the Holocaust memorial in Jerusalem, and is not at all sure that she ever will. It holds mystical meanings that are too strong for her—meanings linked to Jewishness. "I solved the problem of my identity by coming here and being an Israeli," she said. "That's settled. So now I know who I am. Next I want to find out more about what it means."

I STAND AT THE WALL

This is the Western (Wailing) Wall of the Temple. Above me is the Dome of the Rock, where Jesus preached inside the Temple and drove out the money-changers. Here Abraham was prepared to sacrifice Isaac. From this same site, according to the faith of Islam, Mohammed ascended into the heavens.

Now it is sunset on a Friday. The Jewish Sabbath is commencing. Strong electric lights shine on the ancient Wall, whose mighty stones have survived centuries of rains, warfare, sunshine, and siege. I wonder how many men perished as they struggled to raise these massive blocks of stone into their permanent resting places for the ages. Shrubs have long ago taken root here, and birds nest between these stones.

In the immense courtyard before the Wall men and boys dance and sing on this Sabbath observance. Others stand close to the Wall and kiss it. Some people read prayers and softly chant, their heads weaving back and forth in worship.

I learn anew the need in religion of a place where people can come to worship together—a shrine, a sanctuary, an altar, a wall.

The Wall stands naked, its ancient stones eternally open to sun, rain, wind, and the eyes of countless people. Coming close to the Wall, I place my hands upon it and my forehead against it. I find it warm, receptive, and accepting.

The first star of evening has just appeared above my head in the firmament of the Jerusalem sky. Shalom. Shalom.

Jerusalem's three great monotheistic faiths—Islam, Christianity, and Judaism—coexist amid holy places and within the bubbling caldron of Middle East politics.

God's houses in Jerusalem will not close, and the three faiths must go on living with one another for a long time to come.

To propose a summit conference of leaders of the three faiths would raise an immediate stumbling block question: Who are the leaders? The Jews might send the two chief rabbis of Israel, one representing the Ashkenazic branch of the faith, the other the Sephardic. Yet this would shut out any spokesperson from the Diaspora, especially the United States, and exclude Conservative, Reconstructionist, and Reform Judaism from representation. Yet another criticism would come from Jews who consider that the head of the Jewish state is not only a political leader but is automatically—by virtue of being Israel's ranking figure and driving force—a spiritual leader of world Jewry.

Muslims have not had a grand caliph since the end of World War I. The Muslim faith could perhaps be represented by the sovereign of Saudi Arabia, or a person designated by him, and a leading Islamic scholar from El Azar, the renowned university situated on the outskirts of Cairo. Representatives of Christianity might be the pope and the head of the World Council of Churches. But surely there would be a clamor for representation on the part of other Christians on various frontiers far from establishment centers.

BETHLEHEM IS NEAR JERUSALEM

I have sung about it in Christmas carols all my life, seen it depicted in crèches, and read about it in the Gospel: "Jesus was born at Bethlehem in Judea during the reign of Herod."

It is good to see this place, to be here at the site of his birth. For doing so captures the specific nature and content of the fact that the cosmic Christ is also the historical Jesus. He was born here, he grew up in Nazareth, he trod this land where he exercised his ministry of healing and preached repentance and salvation, he was crucified under Pontius Pilate, suffered and died, and he rose from the dead.

"She wrapped him in swaddling clothes, and laid him in a manger, because there was no room for them in the inn."

Today Jesus' birthplace is a shrine that is crowded and commercial. Guides reach out to sell a souvenir or take a tip. Busloads of visitors clog the roads.

In the hustle and bustle, one needs to concentrate very carefully and deeply on the Lord whose birth remains vitally alive in one's faith. "Glory to God in highest heaven, and on earth his peace for men on whom his favour rests."

"During the ceasefire between one war and another, between one terrorist attack and the next, we assemble here, writers from all over the world, in Jerusalem the City of Peace, to discuss 'Cultural Heritage and Creativeness.'" The speaker was Israeli writer Aharon Megged, giving the keynote address for the Thirty-ninth International Congress of PEN (the worldwide organization of poets, essayists, and novelists), which I attended in Jerusalem in December 1974.

Relating language to the congress's theme of cultural heritage, Megged said that "words . . . carry the traits and qualities of peoples, their accumulated experience." He emphasized the importance of Israeli writers' continuing to use inherited Jewish words "that have no accurate translation in any other language: exile, diaspora, pogrom, sacrifice, and, in the last generation, holocaust." Such words, he declared, have not lost their meaning in Israel; "they have only changed color in the new environment which is more open to sun and free air."

The conference raised the question: What power do writers and intellectuals possess? Novelist Saul Bellow said: "Literature is not a power in life. Power is in government, politics, the mass media. The writer has been shut out. He is not at the center of things. Yet one part of mankind is in prison, another is starving to death. Another seems not to be fully awake. What will it take to rouse us?"

Heinrich Böll spoke of this century as "the century of the persecuted" and observed: "We occasionally feel that history is a stranger to us. Not only writers and teachers feel it. Writers and teachers are only luckier in being able to express it."

I WALK AROUND THE WALL OF JERUSALEM

It is a sunny day and I sweat as I climb atop the wall. Now I imagine that I am standing here several thousand years ago. An enemy approaches. Ladders are mounted to take the wall. I crouch behind the stones, clutching a long spear.

But a sound behind me brings me abruptly back to the present time. A man astride his donkey rides by. The donkey looks at me quizzically.

The past and the present are inextricably mixed in my consciousness here.

God remains with me in both.

Fourteen million Jews are alive in the world today. Of these, nearly three million live in Israel. The rest are scattered. It is perhaps natural that most Jews, remembering the death of six million Jews in the Holocaust, are extraordinarily sensitive concerning the survival of Jewish peoplehood and the life of Israel.

"We Jews are like a cancer," an Israeli woman said. "You can wipe us out by the millions as Hitler did. You can kill us in gas chambers. You can push us down into the earth. But then we'll simply come up again somewhere else. You can't ever really destroy us."

THE GARDEN OF GETHSEMANE IS A PARADOX

In this lovely spot nestled at the foot of the Mount of Olives, the agony of Christ spilled over. He said to his disciples: "My heart is ready to break with grief. Stop here, and stay awake with me." But they slept.

Today the Garden seems to contain many mysteries. Near these two-thousand-year-old olive trees Jesus prayed: "My Father, if it is possible, let this cup pass me by. Yet not as I will, but as thou wilt."

Standing inside Gethsemane, I realize how well Jesus has always known human nature and loved people. "What! Could none of you stay awake with me one hour? Stay awake, and pray that you may be spared the test. The spirit is willing, but the flesh is weak."

The weaknesses, fears, and mixed intentions of Christ's followers are never hidden from him, then or now. Judas came into the Garden of Gethsemane to betray Christ.

Disciples who follow Christ today can usefully pause in Gethsemane and ponder the Gospel story that was written about this place. Our human self-assurance needs constantly to be offered to God—to be refreshed and purified.

Past midnight, our conversation took place in a Jerusalem bar that was nearly emptied of people and about to close.

"We must put Auschwitz behind us now," said a prominent European Jewish writer who was once a prisoner in a Nazi concentration camp. "Not speak of it. There has been too much emphasis on both memory and death. It is new life that matters. We shall have to have the courage to live it and no longer look back."

A silence followed her remarks. Then an Israeli writer spoke up in response: "I am too full of feeling to say anything about that. Not now. Maybe sometime."

YAD VASHEM IS THE HOLOCAUST MEMORIAL
IN JERUSALEM

Here the names of the Nazi death camps are inscribed. Jewish victims of the Holocaust are memorialized here. The ashes of some Jewish victims have been brought from the places of their torture to this permanent shrine.

A museum inside Yad Vashem depicts the agony of the Jews in the Holocaust. Sometimes Nazi soldiers took photographs of the obscenities and tortures they perpetrated. A number of these pictures have been preserved and are on exhibit. So we see with our own eyes the lynchings, hangings, and burnings of Jews. Emaciated men, women, and children imprisoned behind bars look out at us. People waiting to be slaughtered gaze at us with longing and wonder.

In the Holocaust memorial at Yad Vashem an eternal flame burns. No sound but a vast stillness permeates the immense stone room. I see Christ crucified in Yad Vashem.

I see Christ crucified in the agony of these people upon whom horror and tortured death were inflicted. "Is it nothing to you, all ye that pass by?" (Lamentations 1:12).

You Jew, Jesus.

On the mornings of two successive Christmas Eves, I was privileged to lead a Christian pilgrimage to the Western Wall. The congregation, standing in the open-air plaza, sang the spiritual "He's Got the Whole World in His Hands." Psalm 96 was read. (It is read in synagogues throughout the world in preparation for the Shabbat). The first line of the psalm—"Sing a new song to the Lord"—was written on a piece of paper and placed in a crevice between the ancient stones on the wall. Publicly, Christians offered thanks for the Jewishness of Jesus.

The quality of Jewish-Christian ecumenical dialogue in America or anywhere else in the world hinges upon the depth of Jewish-Christian meeting in Israel. This does not necessarily mean catching an El Al plane and flying to Israel; it means the depth of a shared consciousness. A consciousness of Israel, the land of the Bible that is shared by Jew and Christian. A consciousness of the Western Wall, Bethlehem, the Via Dolorosa, David's Tomb, and, yes, Yad Vashem. The quality of such mutual comprehension determines whether, and how, Jews and Christians shall be able to meet in Los Angeles, Milwaukee, Atlanta, Chicago, Houston, Cleveland, and New York and anywhere in the world. For Israel means the homeland, the focal point, of Jewish peoplehood. From the womb of this covenanted peoplehood came the Christian faith.

Jews comprise this peoplehood—with roots in religion, history, and culture. A modern Jew is kinsperson to the Hebrew exile who, in 586 B.C.E., cried out: "By the waters of Babylon, there we sat down and wept, when we remembered Zion."

Jesus was neither a Christian nor a Muslim. Jesus was a Jew. There is a particularity here that cannot be dismissed. In order to speak broadly universal concepts, one must work patiently and humbly with particularity. "For out of Zion shall go forth the law, and the word of the Lord from Jerusalem," wrote Isaiah.

WHERE IS THE PLACE OF JESUS' DEATH?

Some say that Golgotha is inside the Church of the Holy Sepulchre; others say it is in the Garden Tomb.

I don't know.

It is easier to meditate in the Garden Tomb with its quiet pathways. Inside the Church of the Holy Sepulchre commercialism is more demanding and rampant, and rich jewels and altar pieces seem distractingly out of place with the bloody wooden cross on which Christ died.

But I would never argue about which place is the correct one. What is essential in my belief is that Christ died for me. I am eternally grateful. His death is for the world. I want the world to understand it.

I wander inside the Garden Tomb. A young woman sits beneath a tree, reading. A man moves ahead of me along the byways and paths. There is peace here.

Later, inside the Church of the Holy Sepulchre, I climb ancient stone stairs down, down, down into a chapel in the very depths of the structure. There is peace here too. "In the world you will have trouble. But courage! The victory is mine; I have conquered the world."

An Israeli friend spoke to me in his apartment.

"I have finally decided that if there is a God, well, damn him," he said. "Can you understand what I feel? If this is the best God can do, and wants to do, then I'm no longer interested." The thirty-year-old Israeli student who spoke with such passion studied law at the Hebrew University, held a white collar job, and had served seven months out of the past twelve in Israel's military reserve.

Late one evening, in November 1974, as I sat across from him, he explained that he had long thought about the question of God. "I deliberately withheld judgment. When I looked at organized religion I saw the bad and the good, all mixed together. I learned to accept this state of affairs, although I had no personal interest at all in religion itself. But now I have come to a decision. Let me explain: My mother escaped from the Nazis and came to Israel from Germany in 1933. She met and married my father here. He was killed in the 1948 war, when I was three years old. I remember the 1956 war, the 1967 war, and the Yom Kippur war. Of course, I fought in the last two. Now many of my friends have died, although I escaped without serious injury. Another war confronts us. They say we are the select people, the chosen people. But chosen for what? To die?"

I LOOK TOWARD THE MOUNT OF OLIVES

Pine trees dot the ravine below. Thousands of Jewish graves appear on the hill.

I walk the length of the wall to a place opposite Gethsemane. Now I climb to the top of the Mount of Olives, past the tombs of Haggai and Malachi. "O Jerusalem, Jerusalem, the city that murders the prophets and stones the messengers sent to her!"

The Chapel of the Ascension is nearby. A guide insists upon pointing out an encased footprint in a stone. He says that it is Christ's footprint at the moment he ascended into the heavens above Jerusalem. But I prefer to have eyes of faith.

The three faiths—Judaism, Christianity, Islam—appear sometimes to be like rare jewels or unparalleled museum pieces kept under glass in the Holy City. What if faith, not grenades, could explode? Can faith in this age shatter hard political presuppositions, a pervasive cynicism, and an expanding malaise of hopelessness?

I FIND MYSELF ON THE WAY OF THE CROSS

Here, Christ began his walk to Golgotha, where he was nailed to the cross, and where he died.

I stand in a church courtyard filled with flowers and ancient trees. Tourists snap photographs with their cameras. Next to us is a church which memorializes the flagellation of Jesus.

After he was flogged, Jesus took up his cross and walked along this road. It is cobblestoned and hemmed in by shops that sell postcards, repair shoes, bake breads, make jewelry, squeeze orange juice, and serve hot meals. So the Way of the Cross is rightly enmeshed in the very fabric of modern human life.

Here, an elderly Arab woman carries a heavy bundle on her head. There, children run and play. A sheep is tied to a nearby iron pipe. Three men sit quietly listening to a radio that blares loud music.

Nearby a barbershop is crowded with men waiting for a haircut. Next to it is a stall that sells apples, cucumbers, and oranges. A small hotel looms ahead. A large sign announces: "VIII Station Souvenir Bazaar."

Finally I reach another chapel on the way. But now I see two other weary pilgrims coming up the road.

"We seem to have lost our way," explains one of them, fatigue masking her face. "We're looking for the Way of the Cross."

Chapter IV

Motion

I feel the motion of abandonment
I am abandoning
I abandon
I yield myself absolutely
I surrender all my inhibitions
I release my chains and claims
I let go of the railing
I trust completely
I give all
I open all the way
I spring
I dive
I fly
I dance
I run
    Laughing
    Yearning
    Praising
    Am I with you?
Am I running with you, God?

HOW CAN I PRAY?

It means to open my life to God—to open my life to others.

AT CHRISTMAS

Save us from being selfish. Help us to give freely and joyfully of
ourselves to others who are in need.

Vivify our thoughts as we recollect the birth of Jesus. May the
poverty of the manger be etched deeply on our consciousness. We
live today in a world still marked by poverty, hunger, and dreadful
need. Grant us compassion and love, Lord, and appreciation that
you share life with us.

AT CHANUKAH

Illumine our consciences, God, with the lighting of the candles
of the Chanukah Menorah. Remind us what Chanukah means
in relation to human freedom, as this is a symbol for all time of
the Jewish struggle for independence and liberty.

Nurture the meaning of Chanukah in our hearts, God. Keep
alive in our souls its meaning for human rights and freedom. Lift
up our eyes. Enable our vision, rooted in memory, gratitude, and
wisdom.

I am in a crowd. I am also standing in a long line. The check-out line in a busy supermarket is long, and I am at the end of it.

Directly in front of me a man stares into space. Canned music plays without ceasing. There is no conversation between people.

I feel indifferent rather than lonely in the crowd. My head has begun to ache. The meaninglessness of the long line stifles curiosity or interest.

The setting is a brightly lit, kinetically active deadness. Although I am numbed by boredom, a core of desperation within me sends signals. In a moment I may shout suddenly, hurl a jar of oregano into the air, or angrily leave my place in the line and stalk out.

No. I must not. Not. Never. No. I must think of the investment of time that I have paid as I moved through the supermarket, up this line, down that line, selecting the items that fill my shopping cart. Not. Never. No.

I must stand very still until I can pay the cashier and walk outside into the crowded parking lot. The canned music plays a show tune about dancing all night and still wanting to dance some more. That is another kind of motion. But now I push my shopping cart forward in the line.

THE MOTION IN HER LIFE STOPPED
A LONG TIME AGO, LORD

She was a young woman, engaged to be married, when she suffered a near-fatal automobile accident. Her body and face were scarred. Her back was critically injured, requiring many operations that finally permitted her to walk again. But she has a permanent limp and needs the assistance of a cane.

Not long after the accident, her fiancé dropped out of her life. He simply went away. After that, she could not find the kind of job that she wanted. Previously she had held a top position in public relations, but her former associates found her presence unattractive and threatening to them now.

People responded to her differently than to the proud and self-consciously beautiful woman she had once been. Soon she became fearful and embittered, withdrawing from activity and even ceasing to try to sort out her life. Her confidence was shattered.

However, at the worst period of her decline, she gradually underwent a change of heart. Her faith and hope were restored. She looked for a job that she could do well and be genuinely interested in as an extension of herself. She found it. She sought involvement with other people, laughed again, managed to put the past behind her, and started to live at a maturer level than she had ever done before. Her interest in other people grew. She opened her life in a completely new way to you, God, and to others.

She learned how to pray with her life, didn't she, Lord?

Fear just moved inside me. Then it halted again. The murderous game of waiting goes on.

This war of attrition is a civil war. It continues without seeming end. The fear inside me faces guerrilla tactics used against it by the terror outside me.

A shadowy motion on the border line of my imagination captures my attention. It is dangerously near the front lines of my will. Shall I use napalm as a defensive action against the terror that invades my life? Nuclear weapons in a first strike at the increasing violence that attacks everything I hold dear and sacred?

In this dark, cold night of my soul, terror and violence lay siege to my deepening fear.

SOMEONE HAS CHOSEN DEATH OVER LIFE, GOD

Someone has murdered helpless people in their apartment in the city at night, and stolen the few dollars they had. This cuts very deep into all of our lives, doesn't it? It is a dread communicable disease.

The victims have been destroyed, their lives wiped out. The family and friends of the victims are caught in a web of helplessness, questioning, and rage.

Yet the murderer is more insidiously infected by the disease. He is, on the one hand, its bearer. But, on the other hand, ultimately he is its victim. For his sensibility rots, his decency spoils, and his sense of worth degenerates into a grotesque image of fake strength and malignant self-pity.

There are more victims: ourselves. We are members one of another in the body of society. Life, goodness, and love are communicable; so are death, evil, and hate. Help us, God, to communicate health instead of disease.

Work as motion filled with meaning is a gift more precious than gold, I have found. But I didn't always feel that way.

At the outset of going to work, I tolerated the work itself and instead waited impatiently for my day's labor to come to an end. I thought that real life began then. Any idea that joy and fulfillment could be found in labor did not occur to me for a single moment.

In the years that ensued, I learned how to build escapes from work into my days. The highlights of my existence became these escapes rather than work, which I continued to regard merely stoically.

Later, I realized that pessimism expressed by a friend of mine rang true for me too. He said: "I keep waiting to live. When do I begin to live? Or is life merely a fantasy? All this work, work, work. I'm so tired."

One day I realized that I was no longer waiting to live. I had begun to live. Life, utterly real, was passing by now fairly rapidly. I loved my work with its demands, human interaction, goals, disappointments, victories, growth, fatigue, and strengths. I found that I was not tired of either my work or life, but vitally interested in them both.

The motion of work places me among the living, for which I am grateful, and separates me from the dead.

NANCY RIDES TO WORK ON A BUS

She lives with her two young children, whose support she solely provides, and her mother, who is ill and unemployed.

It is a nasty day, drizzling and freezing cold, outside the bus window through which Nancy looks.

Many people, observing her life's routine, would feel that it lacks excitement, much hope, or options for improvement of her condition.

Yet Nancy doesn't feel this way at all. After watching her grandmother slowly die of sickness and loneliness in a county nursing home, Nancy is grateful that she can take care of her mother. She delights in her children, their growth and education, and thanks God she has the strength to provide for their needs.

Nancy discovers excitement in the dozens of small challenges and events that make up each day of her life. Hope is not just a word for her. She has translated it into attending night courses in accounting and nursing, which she feels offer fine options for her future.

Right now, her prayer is work. Her work is prayer. And riding the bus to work is one of the prayers in Nancy's day of wonder and joy.

The motion of life asserts its own pace upon us.

If the soul wishes to build Rome in a day, the body knows that the city must be built inch by inch, stone by stone, year by year.

If the soul wishes to achieve human justice without delay, the body knows that hunger needs to be given food, thirst requires water, and the human heart has to be changed in addition to altering laws.

If the soul wishes work to be illumined by high goals and deep meaning, the body knows that conditions of work must include safety, dignity, fairness, equitable compensation, and human rights.

If the soul wishes human love to possess purity and beauty, the body knows that its own hungers have to be satisfied and its own character understood.

As it is a part of human perplexity to be a body and a soul, so this very condition of creation links us one to another. We are all bound together by the social necessities of life—work, sexuality, politics, and human organization. We search for meaning in these, and suffer if we do not find it.

The body and the soul form a single whole, each having to accommodate itself to the reality of the other. This balance is found in the motion of life.

WHAT CAN I MAKE OF THE MOTION OF BUSYNESS?

While a part of it appears to be necessary and good, Lord, another part seems a delusion and bad.

Remaining in a static condition, refusing to function or interact with the rest of life, is surely wrong. I hate falling into a trap where I find myself alienated, aloof, and a stone instead of a human person.

However, busyness that is devoid of meaning beyond itself is just as wrong, I feel, God. It is sad to watch an older person move from such busyness into enforced retirement. The loneliness within activism for its own sake simply remains the same within a protracted idleness.

I want busyness in my life, God, that allows pockets of solitude, elbow room for space, and time laps contrapuntal to running.

A *step at a time.* But I want to pole-vault over the months and years, decisions and events, and be there now. Where? My destination.

But what if I have no destination in the sense that an arrow has a mark? What if I am supposed to learn patience as a faraway goal instead of having any clear place to reach?

It seems that it would be easier to have a destination on a simple road map of the soul's journey. My ego needs would be met more fully that way. I could point to a clearly marked terminal point of life and say, "There it is. I have achieved. I have reached where I set out to go." And, if I wished, I could perhaps also have broken the rules of speed getting there.

However, to learn patience as a goal must be indescribably harder for me. I cannot point toward patience in myself, as I could at an arm or leg on my body, and say, "There it is." Certainly I shan't be able to exclaim, "I have achieved." Indeed, how shall I ever know if I have arrived, circumspectly completed my task, and become qualified to be called a success?

A *step at a time* is the motion that the journey of the soul may require of me.

HE STARES INTO SPACE

I can't help observing him closely, Lord, for he stands directly ahead of me on an escalator that moves slowly, carrying us from floor to floor inside this building.

His thoughts appear to be a thousand miles away from here. Under one arm he carries a large package wrapped in brown paper. Is it a lamp? Breads, cheeses, and wines? A new hose for his garden?

I just caught sight of his face. It strikes me as showing concern. For what, Lord? Is his job in jeopardy? Can I reach out, touch him, and establish human communication with this man? I sense a need in him for support. Can I help him? There is an awful lack of loving concern for others in this impersonal place with its long lines of tired, waiting people.

Lord, are you the man?

WHAT SHALL I DO
WITH MY HUNGER AND THIRST, GOD?

I cry out for wholeness
I accept myself as one small part of your creation, your plan of life
Yet I want to know, understand, and fully share the other parts of
    your life
Now I see through a glass, darkly
But when face to face?
My peace requires union in you
I yearn for this with all my body, all my mind, and all my soul
The inward and spiritual truth that I seek has many outward and
    visible signs that I can comprehend
These signs emerge in the various meanings that love possesses
Ecstasy with you, God, I know in part
I cry out, in my passion and need, for the very wholeness of
    communion with you
I hunger
I thirst
For you

Thank you for loving and nourishing and sustaining me.

Chapter V

Celebration

"*Our life here on earth is a school,*" my mother told me during a talk that we had not long ago. "*Death is a journey with no advance itinerary, maps, or reservations. There is no return. You're just going into an unknown that requires complete faith in God's guidance and direction. I find it exciting.*"

SHE IS EIGHTY YEARS OLD, LORD

My mother's wisdom, accumulated through her lifetime, is a marvel for which I give thanks.

She knows how to cure the common cold by rubbing goose grease on one's chest; prepare a memorable pot of vegetable soup (based on *her* mother's recipe) that cannot be bought with gold in the finest restaurants of New York or Paris; care for the birds that flock to her backyard, tend a rose garden, manage her home; keep up with reading, correspond with friends everywhere, work as a volunteer at a children's hospital; study French and the guitar at a nearby Everywoman's Village; paint, design her Christmas cards; heal back aches and pains by a massage with oils; cherish the company of two faithful dogs; swim six months of the year, reject any onslaughts of depression; dress in impeccable but understated fashion—and always wear a ribbon in her hair; remain loyal to old and new friends, speak her mind directly if sometimes bluntly, care deeply about social issues, volunteer to assist political candidates of her choice; laugh on occasion at herself and everybody else, and show the world a stubbornly happy and smiling face.

Thank you for her life, Lord.

I attended a celebration of a "house church" liturgy in a suburban home. As the bread and wine were consecrated, a Roman Catholic priest and I read alternate paragraphs of the service, and finally we read together. The bread was passed from one person in the circle to the next.

"Jesus Christ," one person said to another. "The body of Christ," said the person on my left. When the wine-filled chalice was passed around the circle (a few drops from it almost fell on the rug when the youth at my right grasped it from my hands), most people announced, "The blood of Christ," to the next person. The exchange of the kiss of peace was energetic, with everyone getting up and managing to kiss and hug everybody else.

I found the liturgy remarkably satisfying. My spiritual needs at that moment—intellectual, physical, emotional—seemed to be fully met. I was fulfilled. I knew that I would likely be turned off by a dryly formal liturgy inside a church building, with a priest or minister in a pronounced "leadership role," a remote high altar, and a crowd of people for whom one felt no immediate relationship in comparison with our intimacy in this setting.

Yet I knew the dangers courted in the house liturgy. A regular habit of this low-key comfort could perpetuate a sameness of being with people whom one simply liked to be with, replacing the tension of compromise and learning patience and humility in the face of difficult relationships. The prophetic voice of the gospel would be stilled, and the needed sense of the universal church wiped out by parochialism.

"This is a way station," someone present at the house liturgy remarked. "It's a temporary solution. The long-range answer hasn't been found yet."

A FAMILY
IS GATHERED AROUND THE DINNER TABLE

Jimmy is late, Lord, and dad somewhat angrily states that *everybody* must be present before grace can be said. Jimmy straggles in, there is a momentary pause, and then dad announces it is Ann's turn to say grace.

"God is great, God is good, and we thank him for our food." She is speaking so hurriedly, one would have to be familiar with the prayer in order to discern it is being uttered. She is also speaking in a deliberate singsong pattern, not at all her natural way of expression. "By his hands we all are fed. Give us, Lord, our daily bread." And then, without taking a breath, culminating the artificial and bizarre performance, she mutters, "Amen."

Everybody sits down around the table, Lord, food is served, and suddenly Ann says something. She is speaking naturally, honestly, and without a trace of her former odd behavior during the grace. The pseudoreligious, baby-twangy rhythm and tone of voice are gone.

Why is prayer ever invoked in such a way, God, as to make it seem altogether meaningless? It seems that people don't realize how attitudes and actions are the essential teaching devices, not words which are contradicted by them. To put it another way: words used in a thoughtless way teach youngsters and other people that the words themselves are not to be taken seriously.

Why is a phony kind of prayer dragged in as magic, or a respectable custom, or because "It's for the kids," Lord? Can't we pray because it is honest and we believe in it—and in you, God?

My birthday is in June.

Because of the moon's position, my horoscope said, I would be subject to great ups and downs in feelings, as well as in a worldly way.

Mercury's being in Gemini would make me perceptive and fluent. My greatest faults would come from too great versatility and lack of application and decision. I would always be torn between two courses of action, said my horoscope.

Indeed, always I have half joked about being a Gemini, for it is true that I cannot choose between two sweaters, neckties, plans, schedules, speaking invitations, book projects, items on a menu, or simple directions.

I SMELL SUMMER'S SWEETNESS

Yet I do not feel ecstasy, Lord. I am heavy. A stone sits upon me. My mind is a mined field, ready to explode.

When I looked in the mirror a moment ago, I saw an alert, fresh face. My eyes appeared to be models of vigor and enthusiasm. How could the mirror tell such an obvious lie? Will other peoples' eyes today be mirrors that lie, too? I don't wish to react nicely to such mirrors.

I am drained of all energy. I don't care whether I live or die, sleep or stay awake, have company or am alone. Nothing interests me. Will I make it through this day? Sweat pours off my body. I am devoid of ambition, caring, or concerns beyond the next five minutes.

However, I also adore this day, Lord. In the lush fullness of the earth, I know a certain lazy contentment. I am pregnant with plans that will require other times and seasons for their fulfillment. I feel them move inside me.

I will sentimentalize this day and long for it on a snowy day next February when the leaves will be dead and the ground frozen.

But now, Lord, I must simply get up. I have to walk from here to there, through the still air into the blazing sunlight.

Inspire me, God.

Autumn means anticipation for me. It is a restless time in which I am also restless.

What is to come? There will be snow and ice, spring and next summer—but what else? Autumn is a signpost that reminds me there is full mystery and the unknown in life. Divine disobedience stirs and moves within my soul.

My life, which has seemingly been progressing in a predictable way upon steady supports, may suddenly swerve in a wholly new direction. I may be called upon to develop new attitudes, relationships, and skills, and even become someone whom I would not recognize now.

So, life is mercurial, dynamic, and changing. Its sometime façade of security and sameness is an absurd delusion.

I welcome autumn and its mood of mystery, its message of change, even its hint of healthy danger.

AN AUTUMN WIND LASHES MY FACE

Trees are shaken. Leaves scatter. Windows rattle.

So much destruction seems to mark my life. Why do I seem to level harm on myself and anyone else who comes too close?

I brutalize life, Lord. I tear savagely at it. I waste it with callous disregard of its sanctity, which is your holy gift. I seem to be close to the edge of a deadly abyss that I can only call despair.

Why do you pursue me, God? Your love confounds me. Why do you stay with me? I am unworthy of your depth of devotion. Yet clearly, you care infinitely.

Autumn is filled with your promise of changes to come. There will be ice. After that there will be rebirth. Hold me close to you. Teach me how to love.

Teach me how to wait in this autumn season, God, for what is to follow in the cycle of your goodness.

The first snowfall came last night. I heard the strange sound of its near silence when I awakened a few moments ago.

Outside my window the world is a fresh vision, with nature acting as the supreme artist. I am grateful for the punctuation mark of this event in my life. The first snowfall is one of my favorite happenings each year.

My eyes feast upon the scene of grace that awaits them. No human or animal tracks yet break the full continuity of fields of snow.

I prepare to walk outside the house and embrace the fresh snow. I will hold it in my hands, rub it upon my face, let it melt in my mouth, and walk through soft drifts of it with my feet. Mostly I will hold its unparalleled beauty in my eyes. I love it deeply and intensely.

What a challenge it is to make tracks with my feet in the freshly fallen snow. It is symbolic of the marks that, inescapably, I must make upon life itself simply because I am alive. I touch other people's lives, the very quality of life, and the whole universe in microcosm, as I add days, months, and years to my human existence.

Let my marks upon life be gentle ones. Oh, may my tracks in fresh snow and upon life be friendly and good.

SNOW FALLS ON A WINTRY DAY

I walk through deep drifts of it. Shapes of black trees are placed in a regimental design of Manichaean contrast to the dazzling play of light on the pure white cover of the earth.

Why, Lord, do I seem to stand outside my life as well as in it? How can I bear to watch myself slowly kill me? I do not want to kill ideals, love, meaning, and hope. Why don't I know better?

Who is the other part of me, the curious stranger who walks in and out of my life, God? Sometimes he mocks me. Other times he is very serious. Then, half laughing, half crying, he wears an inscrutable face as he hurts me really quite badly. I want the stranger to go away, Lord, or else become my friend and stay quietly with me.

A distant frozen sun hangs in the sky as if it were a stranger there. I am alert. My mind races. My body moves swiftly in instinctive fast motions to increase circulation and so survive.

I long for the hot sun to bring warmth to the unyielding cold of the earth.

Warm me, God.

The miracle has happened again. Yesterday the air was still bitingly cold, with not the least suggestion of a change to come. Today the air possesses the seductive warmth of love.

There is more evidence of the miraculous. When I went walking just now, I saw emerging buds. I could swear they were not visible yesterday.

I know, of course, that spring does not last. What shall I do with it during these brief, splendid days that fall between the end of winter and the coming of summer? I am content to move or stay silent in its embrace, breathe its wondrous smell, and let the world stop for us.

But it will not stop. Spring will quickly pass. So will I, running briefly across the space of earth and through time. Spring fills me with gratitude for all of life and my own, its brevity being like that of my years in the span of God's ages.

SPRING IS SO BRIEF, LORD

Its tenderness touches my thick skin. Its perfume delights my jaded senses. Its promise stirs up the milk of goodness in me that I thought had dried up.

Is spring's brevity like that of my own life in the span of your ages, God?

Stretch my life to the very limits of love, God.

Chapter VI

Justice

In cruel moments when injustice seems to reign triumphant over human affairs, and tyranny stifles people's instinct for freedom, one hears the cry: Why doesn't God do something?

God does not cause world horrors; we do. As co-creators with God in the ever-continuing action of creation, we are called to use our own bodies, spirits, and minds and to work with God.

God did not bring Jesus down from the cross or tranquilize him in the throes of his suffering. God did not hurl a thunderbolt from on high to disrupt Nazi trains carrying victims to death camps. God does not still the guns of war or coerce torturers to cease to inflict the lash. God does not stop cruel mistreatment of the poor and disenfranchised, for God expects us to do this as well as to change the underlying conditions that lead to such mistreatment.

As co-creators with God, we have our creative work to do.

DARE WE REMAIN SILENT, GOD?

Open our ears to cries of pain. Open our hearts to each other's needs. Open our eyes to social as well as personal sin. Open our mouths to speak your words of love and justice in order to break open a silence of tyranny. May we witness to these our words, Lord, with our lives that seek to follow your will.

I am worried, really worried, about the serious deterioration in relations between blacks and whites.

Black friends share their sense of frustration and anguish with me. Some hold a bleak vision of the future of urban black masses. "I look around me and see lost black people," one friend told me. "Many blacks are committing their own genocide inside their heads and guts. You can almost hear the sound of psychic explosions."

I find myself, in gatherings of whites, suddenly baffled by the level of conversation: "What would you do if you were walking down the street and you saw two black men walking toward you?" (Answer: "Cross the street.") Or, "What would you do if you were in an elevator that stopped at a floor to admit two black men?" (Answer: "Get out.")

Time may be running out for all of us. A striking biracial example and witness at this time, when there is a diminution of emphasis upon civil rights and the cause of racial justice, could be a positive means of generating hope and renewed determination.

A lot of people are tired and discouraged. Can we become awakened to the salvific vision of justice and hope, and spur ourselves to needed action?

STRENGTHEN US, GOD

We are selfish
We turn our backs on the needs of others
We are timid
We do not wish to rock the boat
We have eyes to see, yet do not see
We have ears to hear, yet do not hear
We have mouths to speak, yet do not speak
We are afraid
We often wish you to go away and leave us alone,
    so that we will not have to become involved
Awaken us from the sin of indifference
Startle us out of the sin of languor
Strengthen our bodies to be instruments of your mercy
    and justice, God
Strengthen our minds to be instruments of your mercy
    and justice, God
Strengthen our wills to be instruments of your mercy
    and justice, God

"Success is how you feel when you get up in the morning," a man seated at the next table said. "You can't predict it. All day people either say 'yes' or 'no' to you. If they say 'yes,' you're an instant success."

The scene outside the window through which I looked shifted abruptly. I was seated atop a hotel in one of America's major cities, eating breakfast in a revolving rooftop restaurant. I felt omniscient as my overview of the city continuously changed. A glass-sheathed building came alongside and a luxury hotel passed by.

Next the city's mammoth complex of expressway lanes loomed into view. A huge green sign below announced "Civic Center." There were few cars today. In the distance I could see smoke pouring out of giant smokestacks. The homes of industrial workers and their families surrounded these smokestacks, which rose haphazardly into the corrupted sky. If one lived in the midst of that scene, what kind of air would be breathed? It was a vision of Dante's hell, with smoke persistently hugging the ground.

The revolving rooftop restaurant maintained its inexorable and relentless turning.

Suddenly a coolly luxurious executive office building drew so close that I believed I could reach out and touch it with my fingers.

I gazed at a building with an art-deco glass façade. A man astride a bicycle seemed to drive into the building and disappear. Did I perceive an apocalyptic scene inside the shifting dreams contained in those reflected walls? What would that shell look like if its glass were smashed? Rage could muster itself for such destruction. There seemed to be no smog or industrial smoke over here; it was concentrated in the industrial sector marked by smokestacks in the distance over there where poor people lived.

WHAT DID JESUS DO TO CHANGE THE WORLD?

He proved that the spirit is the mightiest force in the world and can break the power of empires.

He elected the failure of the cross and made a farce of the world's measure of success in comparison with it.

He showed people forever that moral power is a greater force than the throne, the scepter, or any other symbol of worldly power.

He proved by the manner of his death that one can be a prisoner or a slave at the hands of men and still be free, for one is a free soul.

He revealed by his resurrection that the kingdom of God is more powerful than the greatest force in the world.

He resolved not to bend to the power of the world, but staked everything on the moral power of God.

Help us, God, to respond to power as Jesus did.

The stench of urine fouls the air in this nursing home, where elderly people wait to die. The sound of TV sets is turned to a maximum level and kept there, like a monstrous distraction from violated human feelings.

Some of the residents in the home are secured to their beds or chairs, others simply tranquilized in a perpetual state of semisleep. Personal care is at a minimum, so a high percentage of the residents suffer from bedsores.

One elderly woman threw herself out of bed in order to break her hip, so that she might be able to die and get out of here. Another elderly person suffered for two weeks with a broken hip before it was diagnosed and he received treatment.

The daughter and son-in-law of the elderly woman who broke her hip are not far away. Their children are grown and have moved, so they live alone in a large, well-furnished home with two empty rooms. She is at home alone most of the time—and could easily take care of her mother there.

The son and daughter-in-law of the elderly man whose hip was broken, and who did not receive proper treatment for two weeks, are also close by. They have an unused extra room in their pleasant home; the daughter-in-law is not employed. But they do not wish to be bothered. To take care of the old man would represent, in their view, an intrusion in their lives, although they have no children.

YOU HAVE INSTRUCTED US, GOD

We have learned from you that we should treat others
    as we would have others treat us.
Why is this one of the most difficult lessons in all
    of life for us to comprehend?
We continue to withhold love.
We deny mercy.
We steel ourselves against compassion.
Most of us will one day grow old, God.
Will we then be treated with love, mercy, and compassion?

In the sixth chapter of the Book of Isaiah, after God has said to Isaiah, "Go—," he instructs the prophet what he must go and say to the people among whom he dwells.

The message is a hard one. There is little optimism contained in it, and certainly no softness. The prophet is to go and proclaim to a rebellious, stony-hearted, and self-loving people the fact that they stand under holy judgment. It is an uncompromising judgment. There is no "Santa Claus" theology in it. It is clear, direct, simple, to the point, and one may not squirm away from its certainty.

When Jesus came to Nazareth and read the scriptures in the synagogue there, he opened to these words in the Book of Isaiah:

"The spirit of the Lord is upon me,
    because he has anointed me to preach good news to the poor.
He has sent me to proclaim release to the captives
    and recovering of sight to the blind,
    to set at liberty those who are oppressed,
    to proclaim the acceptable year of the Lord."

O GOD

>Make us aware of new ways instead of the old ruts
>This is our prayer

O God

>Lift us out of self-hatred and despair
>This is our prayer

O God

>Help us to offer honest and deep thanks for life with you and
>all the other people
>This is our prayer

O God

>Teach us how to make our prayers and lives become the same
>This is our prayer

O God

>When our world chooses death over life, show us how to
>choose life over death
>This is our prayer

O God

>Life over death. Our prayer is for life over death. Life over
>death, God. Life over death
>This is our prayer

O God

>Life over death

Society tends to define people's humanity according to its labels and their images. Henceforth no deviation is expected from stereotypes of "woman," "man," "black," "gay," "Chicano," "Indian," "Jew," "Christian," and indeed "wop," "dago," "chink," "gook," and on and on. A great many people have settled for such a public role, accommodating themselves to its limitations and offering a long performance on a constant public stage. They forever watch other people react to a persona and not a person.

But tyranny has come close when people dutifully play given unhappy roles, wear prescribed crushing masks, speak lies (including a central one concerning their own humanity), and, having honored the demands of society to the end, die in slavery. God wants people who are created in his image to be free.

Why does being "different" threaten other people to the point that they will war against it? The Star of David, a sacred symbol of Judaism, was transformed into a mark of death by the Nazis. Synagogues were put to the fire, Jewish homes looted, property confiscated, and millions of people systematically destroyed because they were "different." Nonwhites have suffered the most monstrous outrages because they were "different"; and so, on other occasions, have white people. Sexual suffering in the world's history is not even capable of being measured. For example, countless women were burned as witches in the Middle Ages. A quarter of a million gay people went to their deaths in Nazi concentration camps. Suffering has so often been inflicted upon people who were "different." They refused, or were unable, to conform to the demands of society.

SHE IS A FIGURE IN MY CHILDHOOD MEMORIES

I remember her as a vital, beautiful, highly talented young woman. She befriended me when I was a lonely, hurting child. I felt unattractive and unloved at that moment in time. Exceptionally supportive and generous with her time, she seemed genuinely to like me.

I felt accepted as a real person. In her eyes I caught a glimpse of my own potential adulthood, and anticipated its coming with a degree of hope.

But I sensed intuitively that she was in trouble. An aura of vague, unnamed criticism surrounded her presence. Finally someone told me, ominously and fearfully, that she was a "Lesbian." I had not heard that word before. It was made to sound like a bad word. I realized, however dimly, that she suffered societal discrimination and persecution as well as considerable emotional anguish. Although she seemed to accept herself, obviously society did not accept her.

I can remember how I worried about the pressure of the pain that was forced upon someone who had unselfishly befriended me and whom I loved.

Why do some people wish to inflict this kind of pain upon other people, God, and justify their actions by saying that they do it in your name?

Prayer needs to be seen as action and a life style. Most prayers we actually live out, in our various relationships. That certainly shows everybody our definition of prayer: whether it is understood as acting out a love relationship with God and our fellow humans, or not.

When I am honest, I strive to say to God: "Your will be done." God's will is for justice, fulfillment, love, dignity, forgiveness, and purpose. The opposite is injustice, hate, degradation, pride, and chaos.

From the human side of it, prayer reaches its greatest meaning. I believe, when the life of the pray-er, and the prayer that is uttered or meant, become one. The response then catches up a whole life in its intensity and conviction. Too, the life then shows marks of unity, no longer revealing a gulf between religious observance on the one hand and the rest of life on the other.

O GOD

What about the hungry people?
How shall they eat and drink?
O God
What about the people held unjustly in jails?
How shall they become free?
O God
What about the children who are abused?
How shall they know liberty?
O God
What about the growing gap between the people who have
and the people who have not?
How shall this gap be closed?
O God
What about the minority people who suffer discrimination?
How shall they come to fullness of life?
O God
What about the elderly who are treated inhumanly?
How shall they know dignity and love?
O God
We your people ask you

Chapter VII

Phony or True

Everything is jumping
Everyone is running
In seven-league boots and sneakers
Barefoot, in boots and shoes and sandals
On tracks, avenues, and hills
Inside trains, buses, cars, and jets
How come?
Everything is moving
Everyone is racing
Through revolving doors and jobs
Into love, out of love
Up to the top, down to the bottom
Don't have a minute
Got a sec?
Everything is flying
Everyone is hustling
Lights, camera
Action, crime, politics
New nations, oceans, moons
Vitamins and meditation, and hey
Look who's here!
Everything is jumping
Everyone is running
Fast

But I've got to stop

SHE LIVES BY HER SCRIPT

The confusions that she reveals are as unreal as the so-called hidden strengths, Lord. Following a second drink, when she looks levelly at another person and makes a stark confession about herself, she has already moved into one of her several fantasy worlds.

She juggles friendships expertly, so friends and fantasy worlds never overlap. People cannot meet to compare intelligible notes about her. Her smile is somewhat blurred, but most people sympathetically find it only soft. Her speech pattern, based on highly individual mental shorthand, is laced with argot. Men tend not to follow it at all literally, hearing only a voice that is universally classified as sexy.

If only, she says to herself, she could make decisions about the things that matter. Just a single decision, as a matter of fact: the right one. This seems to be further away from her now than ever before.

However, there is always the script to follow. She wrote it when she created the character for herself. To thine own character be true, she says, and gets a laugh.

Now she is talking on the telephone. Her pretty blurred face breaks into a soft smile. She says a few words, wondering what they meant. Reassured by the voice on the other end of the line, she responds with a slurred laugh. Yes, she will be glad to have dinner with him tonight.

Will she ever discover herself, Lord?

Success and failure are interchangeable.

Unforgettably I learned this on New Year's Eve 1949, when the arrest of Charles Chaplin, Jr., on a charge of drunken driving banished world news from the headlines of newspapers. I remember the occasion very well because I was a friend of Chaplin and, indeed, the other occupant of his car at the time of the arrest. I worked in Hollywood as a television producer.

Why did a minor automobile mishap dominate the front pages? Because Charles Chaplin's son had been arrested. In the fiercely hostile environment of the pre-McCarthy period in the United States, Charles Chaplin was attacked as a "Red," a figure in a sensationally publicized paternity suit, a "foreigner," and a chastised fallen idol.

Yet Chaplin had not long been Hollywood's greatest success and the premier film star in the world. Chaplin's film self, the Tramp, told millions of people about their own humanity; The Great Dictator laughed at the Hitler myth, dissecting it; but later Monsieur Verdoux confronted, and infuriated, people who took themselves too seriously. "My prodigious sin was, and still is, being a nonconformist," Chaplin said.

I recall chatting with Chaplin after his son's arrest. He was dapper, even elegant. His sophisticated clown's face was vulnerable in its sensitivity, revealing sadness as well as uncomprehended hurt. Not long afterwards, Chaplin left the United States and went to live in Europe. As the years passed, so did the acrimonious catcalls. Charles Chaplin's reputation as an artist in the cinema is secure.

But I learned how ephemeral success is when I watched Charles Chaplin suffer, wearing the public label of a failure.

THE YOUNG MAN KNOWS THAT ONE DAY
HE WILL BE THE PRESIDENT

But now he is an assistant learning the business from the bottom up, Lord.

He has a great advantage because he never threatens anyone. He's always The Kid, and can do no wrong so long as he stays strictly inside that role.

When the older executives treat him paternalistically, he smiles boyishly and wins their further admiration for his humility. This is considered a wholesome virtue. When the same people are mean to him if he walks too far into the line of office fire, he makes them feel guilty by his mien of long-suffering innocence.

Meanwhile, he dates the young secretaries, has long ago learned from them where most of the skeletons are hidden in the closets of the executives' private lives, and has his eye on the top job.

Will he be as nice to people on their way down, God, as they are to him on his way up?

The paradoxes of success and failure remain unknown to him. He does not yet understand to what extent success can be failure, failure can be success.

A *nice prayerful warm glow is conveyed by the announcer who signs off the radio late at night with the words "Peace be with you." What does he mean by that? If he means "May you be tranquilized," he doesn't mean peace in any serious biblical or theological sense. A famous hymn refers to Jesus' disciples in this way:*

> *Contented, peaceful fishermen,*
> *Before they ever knew*
> *The peace of God that filled their hearts*
> *Brimful, and broke them too.*

What kind of peace is the late-night announcer talking about? Is it false "peace"—ingrown, uninvolved, denoting personal security, and hang other people's problems?

Religion does, in fact, become an opiate of the people if prayer is reduced to rote magic and a heartfelt supplication that life remain fundamentally the same as it has always been, without social changes or shattering new insights to boggle the mind and stir the spirit. This isn't saying to God, "Your will be done." Instead, it's saying, "My will be done, with Your blessing." And this is more than phony. It is really blasphemy when it means playing a perpetual childish game with God.

SHE HAS $10,000,000

However, she might be better off if she had to catch an early bus in the mornings in order to reach a distant job.

She will not be awake this morning when her maid arrives for work. In fact, the worst moment in her day is the first one upon awakening, when she faces the emptiness of existence.

It isn't, of course, that she has nothing to do, Lord. She is on a dozen symphony and art-museum committees for big donors, and is a main contributor to a nearby posh church that she attends without fail once each year on Easter morning. Then she wears a bright new spring outfit and is the very picture of tranquil devotion.

Daily she lunches with friends at the country club or any smart restaurant of their choice. She can fly on an instant's notice to Los Angeles, London, or Hongkong.

Yet all the therapy in the world hasn't given her a motivating reason to face another day. A pragmatist, she got off liquor a long time ago and resolutely stayed off it. Boredom is the enemy. She has known a lot of men, mostly the husbands of friends, and honestly, honey, she doesn't give a damn about that route.

Her husband walks through his own paces, which meet hers in the midst of yet another social gathering. Her children are away at school (thank God, she says) and growing up rapidly. They are strangers who smile handsomely when they hold their hands out for more dough.

God, she wishes that something mattered.

Politics and religion, recurring bedmates, come close together every four years during U.S. presidential elections.

Suddenly, candidates running for office who have not darkened the door of a church for a decade are earmarked by their publicists as veritable candidates for canonization. Obscure clergy are brief media celebrities when they are photographed with presidential hopefuls at the conclusion of Sunday religious services near whistle stops.

British Prime Minister Winston Churchill provided a refreshing variation when he arrived on a Saturday night by ship in New York from London. Asked by reporters where he would attend divine services the next morning, Mr. Churchill candidly announced that he would be found resting in his bed.

But American politics allows little candor when it comes to the subject of religion. As a Hollywood star seems to work harder while attending a cocktail party than anywhere except on a movie set, so does a presidential contender seemingly engage in harder campaign work inside God's house than anywhere but the depths of precincts.

All candidates could well choose to address issues from a broad moral base rooted in Judeo-Christian ethics. But when a politician publicly invokes a special association with either the Hebrew prophets or Christ, it is inescapably suggested that goodness uniquely rubs off on him.

The hard truth is that one politician shares moral ambiguities with the rest of the candidates, as well as relative approximations of justice, love, and truth itself. A candidate who understands these things, and honestly acts upon their political implications, is indeed marked as the possessor of a profound religious virtue: godly humility.

YOU KNOW WHAT IS PHONY OR TRUE, LORD

And what is in the middle ground where most people live.

Steer us away from the phony, particularly when it is a part of ourselves, God.

SOMETIMES PEOPLE SEE THEMSELVES AS GODS

The harm and destruction that people who do that have been known to wreak on others is incalculable, isn't it?

Save us from the power of these people, Lord, especially if they also believe strongly in their own sincerity.

How can one cut through images that have been fabricated concerning another person in order to find the reality of that person?

I remember how people in Citizen Kane set out to research a well-known man, yet utterly failed to find him underneath millions of lines of newsprint or in the recollections of his close friends. The reality of the man, locked inside the word "Rosebud" painted on a child's sled, eluded them.

The struggle to be a person instead of a persona is a complex one that concerns not only the great names of the world but all of us.

Once a magazine assigned a writer to spend several weeks with me in order to write an interview. I assumed that he would put two and three together, weigh inconsistencies on a trusty antique scale, and compare my objective lucidity on one occasion with my uncoolly subjective response to an angry verbal attack on another. I thought he would catch my assorted moods, observing me wrapped in a happy disposition (at least in a sunny clime) or shrouded in introspective gloom (anyhow, caught in the rain).

The published interview disappointed me. It seemed to me that a dimensionless image emerged, albeit as stuffed with ersatz charisma as a Christmas stocking with bright loot. A persona was present in the magazine story, but not a person. It made me sad when I went searching for myself. I didn't find me.

EXPLOITATION TERRIFIES ME, GOD

It is such an easy thing to do. In our world, it is a way of life.

We manufacture sexiness, packaging it like bars of soap. We lock people into any kind of a mold that we like, limiting one another's freedom. We let celebrities deliberately lock themselves and us into all sorts of unyielding iron masks, throwing away the keys that could open them up.

We pose behind a myriad of social roles, refusing to meet others as people, and not giving an inch in our determination to simply place images in conflict with other images.

Yet neither public nor private morality can be a posture, can it, Lord? Any morality must surely be an outward expression of one's deepest faith and meaning.

Why does our world believe in justification by the media, Lord, instead of justification by faith in you?

Spiritual hunger that persists in the lives of people is as strong a drive as genital hunger. Organized religion has long repressed it. It has too often placed a tight lid on spirituality that is independent or nonconformist in comparison with its own choreographed dogma-cum-ritual. So, it has left people adrift by forcing upon them answers-cum-authority to questions they never asked.

The deep and pervasive spiritual hunger in many people lies near the surface of their lives. But not until they are half drunk on a rainy night, or caught off guard by a severe crisis, do they often want to discuss it.

Despite invariable sophistication in matters pertaining to their work, sex, and culture, they are religiously tightly locked up inside an Early Sunday School Era classroom. These people inevitably say that God is love. Yet they clearly are torn between utter disbelief in God on the one hand and a lurking superstitious fear, "What if God should exist?" on the other. Indeed, this fear is sometimes treated as if it were a cobra nestled alongside a martini pitcher. Why?

The answer is apparently rooted in guilt that is traced back to one's earliest instruction about God. Everywoman was Eve. Everyman was Adam. The Garden of Eden was innocence. It has turned into a prefiguring of hell, whether or not one believes in a hell.

IF I TOLD THE TRUTH
A LOT OF PEOPLE WOULD BE HURT, GOD

I would be hurt, too.

Does it really make any difference whether or not I tell the truth? The whole thing is way in the past. Nothing can be done about it now.

In fact, isn't telling a lie in a case like this actually an act of love? People, including myself, are spared pain. Hard issues are not opened up. Conflict and controversy are averted. Sweetness and light are maintained, or at least the outward appearance of them.

What is truth, Lord? There are truths all over the place, it seems to me. But truth itself is staggering. I am tempted, I realize, to define truth according to simply what I want it to be.

Why can't I remain a contented phony, Lord? Must your truth force me to tell the truth?

Chapter VIII

The Long Run

*I carry a card in my billfold that gives these clear instructions:
"I hereby make this anatomical gift, if medically acceptable, to
take effect upon my death. I give any needed organs or parts for
the purpose of transplantation, therapy, medical research or education. This is A Legal Document Under The Uniform Anatomical Gift Act." I have signed the card.*

*This is a concrete symbol of my comprehension of death's
demand upon me. It is a part of life's demand, too. I have neither
a morbid fear nor a clear understanding of death. I am convinced
that, following the cremation of my physical remains, the person
who I am will continue to live, but in ways that are now beyond
my ability to comprehend.*

DEATH IS SUCH A DEEP MYSTERY TO ME

Certain elements of the sheer human finality of it I acknowledge without reservation. A long-standing regret of mine concerns a quite elderly friend, a remarkably sensitive and agile gentleman who ran an art gallery. He would have greatly enjoyed my taking him out one day for a late and long lunch, with a carafe of wine and many courses of conversation. I didn't, Lord. I became too busy and forgot, until I was notified that he had died. My opportunity had died too.

I remember well a morning at the end of a long train ride which carried me to my father's funeral, God. As a newly ordained priest, I planned to conduct the final rites. It seemed the last earthly thing I could do for him.

Amid the last preparations which quickly hastened toward their conclusion, people surged around me. I looked for a long moment into my father's painted face in the open casket. The face was a mask. My father had departed, Lord. I saw instead distorted images of my pain, loneliness, and now everlasting sense of loss.

Unravel death's mystery for me, God.

Before my final death, please help me to die a hundred, a thousand, ten thousand times to my pride and isolation, greed and self-will, so that I may bear the scars of such deaths as signs of eternal life with you.

The world is, I find, neither a diagramed globe in the corner of my study nor even reality out there. Sometimes I seem to carry it on my shoulders, while its explosions and cries echo inside the whirling universe of my own mind. Other times I seem to wander aimlessly inside it, scaling its heights and exploring its valleys.

I do not feel that it is possible, barring a lobotomy of one's sensitivities and feelings, to "get away from it all." I do not want to "get away from it." The concept of "peace of mind," sadly exploited by spiritual hucksters, disturbs me. Any selfish attempt to "escape" from human realities is doomed by moral as well as pragmatic facts of life. It becomes a denial of the beauty and meaning of life.

Yet restoration of self is a recognized necessity. I must find wholeness in the relation between the world and me, between God and me.

I have experienced God in the ordinariness of life more than in its variegated complexity. In the form and unity of the seasons, the week, the month, the night, the noon, the day. In those friendships where there was the give and take of intimacy, shared failures and triumphs as the world or the heart calls these things, and the utmost human support at moments when life's very structure seemed to sway uneasily as if it would crash.

Intimacy. The sharing that can be contained in a glance, a touch, a single string of spoken words, a declaration of what had been forever unknown to anyone else, when one joins in the perplexity, assurance, pain, and joy of another person.

ROBERT LIES IN A HOSPITAL BED

Life goes on around him. Other patients fill remaining beds, receiving help from doctors and nurses who pursue their tasks.

Robert knows that he is dying. He struggles to pull all of life into the center of his pain, existence, and fulfillment. He momentarily finds himself very much alone.

Seconds ago, he started to recite the words of the Lord's Prayer, recollected from childhood. Fragments of the prayer fell into place. But his strength has departed.

A new awareness comes over Robert that his dead-center aloneness is shared with the presence of God. He perceives the Lord to be his closest Companion and Friend. Robert's need of words in order to communicate is gone. He is aware that the Lord supports and holds him.

Robert breathes with difficulty. He gently laughs with God, and his face resembles a child's in trust and easy joy. Robert's breath is a prayer. God receives the prayer.

I have felt physical pain so intense that I could scarcely draw a breath or make the slightest move without suffering outrageous agonies. The situation seemed both intolerable and hopeless. At the end of night, I could tell by the hint of light in the sky outside my window that another day of dread repetition was on the horizon.

What to do? I learned how to pray into the pain. I perceived that I must move through the full impact of it before I would be liberated from the pain. This meant letting go. My resistance to the pain was an absurdity, a stoical act of megalomania. I had to move with the pain, and let myself be taken where it led me. So, pain and I became intimate friends.

This reminds me of how someone whom I know reacted to the painful death of a loved one. He played, over and over and over, a recording of the song "Let It Be." The reiteration of this statement of hope, and its signal of light being found in heavy darkness, became an act of healing for his grieving and wounded spirit.

This was not an escape from the knowledge of his loss. This was not a distraction from his pain. But his spirit moved directly into the pain, and through it, to a haven of relief. There came a glimmering of personal understanding to assist his consciousness of presently unbearable loss.

MALCOLM BOYD

CRIES OF PAIN ENCIRCLE THE WORLD

There are cries of hunger, dying, anxiety, torture, loneliness, brutality, depression, self-concern, and a sense of anguish for the suffering of others.

I do not want to be shielded from the terror and volume of so many cries of pain, Lord. My partnership with you in creation means that I must somehow be able to hear these cries, too, and absorb their meaning into my life.

If I only hear such cries of pain, and do nothing about alleviating their cause, I betray you, don't I, God?

I walked randomly on a hot Sunday morning within an inner city. I experienced a vast, mysterious, and chilling emptiness. Some streets were without a human being or a vehicle as far as my eye could see. Occasionally I identified a few Giacometti-like human figures. A person sat, head in hands, in front of a closed library. An elderly man, hat pushed partially over his face, slept on his back in the grass of a small park where Muzak-like music poured through loudspeakers.

A single car appeared, moving at first slowly in the distance. It came close and passed me. On a line of benches facing a boulevard sat four white men, each one occupying a private bench. All of them looked straight ahead. No one spoke.

I saw a church. Four or five elderly people entered it. Its sermon topic was printed on an outdoor bulletin board. "Where Do You Think You Are Going?"

Soon I found myself in the midst of an urban renewal area where buildings had been demolished. It looked like Berlin after World War II. I continued to walk, coming to a wide boulevard with a red traffic light.

Now a large car sped toward the intersection. I waited. As the car passed by, its four passengers looked at me for a moment. I saw a mixture of disdain and utter emptiness in their eyes. Riding in a large, fast-moving, air-conditioned car through the hot streets of the empty city on this Sabbath morning, they seemed to belong to a remote super race. Quickly they disappeared from my sight. A solitary figure who walked the barren streets in anonymity, I was a creature outside of their mind.

SAVE US FROM ISOLATION, GOD

We need to communicate with each other across abysses of separation.

How can we let you enter into our lives, Lord, if we shut out our sisters and brothers who share the earth with us?

From the bitterness and loneliness of keeping you and other people outside our lives, save us, God. Nurture in us your love of the whole of life that you have created.

Let us be faithful followers of your way of responsibility, unselfish involvement in your people wherever they are found, and love, God.

I have known God longer than anyone else in my life. As a child, I knew instinctively that I could rely on God, who was clearly not indifferent to my feelings. Nor did he betray me to utter grief.

It was Sunday School that completely garbled my thoughts about God. In the first place, the teachers there took him away from me. They put God on mountaintops, doing all kinds of dramatic put-on things. Suddenly God was unreachable, a superstar with an uncontrollable ego, a penchant for magic, and a corps of press agents who ran the church.

Jesus seemed to be a nice man. He was young, white, liked animals (pictures on the walls of my Sunday School classroom depicted him as a shepherd), and everybody was fond of him.

Christmas became lovely because of Jesus. He had been born in a manger. Always on Christmas Eve I now empathized with Jesus in his birth, although I was no longer a baby and my comfortable home was not a manger. But the angels singing, the shepherds crowding around, the star shining in the night sky, Joseph and Mary locked in a circle of light with the infant Jesus, were pictures beautiful beyond belief that could make my heart beat fast and draw hot tears to my eyes.

I was determined to surprise Santa Claus with his reindeer when they lit upon the roof of my house. (Surely they would make enough noise to awaken me.) Yet I always failed to confront Mr. Claus. Who could he be? Apparently he was pure beneficence. I never confused him with God. While Santa Claus capriciously visited only once each year, and even then did not wish to communicate, God was a constant friend for 365 days.

YOURS IS THE FABRIC OF LIFE, GOD

The interwoven relationships, the give and take, warp and woof, tension and release, ups and downs that are inseparable from the tapestried existence of life all come together in your will and creation, God.

I believe that the heart of life can be found in this pattern, Lord, if one consents to be patient and seek it gently. Some seekers turn away from the search with distraught fatigue and a belief that a sophisticated crossword puzzle has somehow eluded their ability to solve it. But the pattern is deceptively simple, isn't it, Lord?

Blessed are the poor in spirit, those who mourn, and the meek, who shall inherit the earth.

Those who hunger and thirst for righteousness will be satisfied.

The merciful will obtain mercy.

The pure in heart will see God.

The peacemakers will be called daughters and sons of God.

Those who are persecuted for righteousness' sake, following the prophets, will know a just and great reward, but not of this world.

Help us to be the salt that does not lose its taste and saltiness, Lord.

Let our light so shine that people may see our good works and give glory to you, God.

Help us to love our enemies and pray for those who persecute us, God.

How to witness prophetically to the Word of God was not taught very well in the theological seminary that I attended before being ordained an Episcopal priest. Instead, we learned how to keep church records, handle monies, instruct youth, preach, administer sacraments, engage in community public relations, maintain church property, and raise funds. Rough edges on students generally gave way to finishing touches that produced "gentlemen" (there were then no women priests) of the church. "Gentlemen," it was implicitly understood, would neither rock boats too hard nor throw any but safe rocks at the Establishment.

One day I realized suddenly that everybody wasn't fond of Jesus at all, despite sentimental churchly tinsel-wrapping of myths. Lent and Good Friday showed how deeply Jesus Christ suffered. The cross on the altar was draped in purple, finally in black. Jesus' body was a bloody carcass covered by flies, hung on a cross to which it was nailed. On Easter Jesus Christ rose from the dead and left the empty tomb. He had died for me, I was told. He forgave my sins. I wasn't too sure what my sins were.

I found out. Yet too often I was taught that my sins were personal ones, lacking social dimensions. So I became obsessed with the sinfulness of my pride—this, a curious contradiction—and overlooked such monstrous evil as the sinfulness of torture as a demonic device practiced increasingly by modern governments against people. Then I heard the bell toll not simply for the victims of torture but for all of us, and for me.

I realized that there is no "personal gospel." There is no "social gospel." The true gospel embraces both personal and social dimensions of sin, salvation, and life itself.

HOW IS IT POSSIBLE TO SURVIVE, LORD?

There seems to be infinitely more that I shall have to survive. Yet I am not doing very well now. Any effort that I make seems so clearly insignificant. I am told by everybody that I cannot change anything for the better in a serious way. A blanket of icy indifference beckons me to lie down upon it and simply go to sleep.

Why bother? Why fight? Why struggle?

Because I want to survive, God. I know that if I am not committed to hope inside my own life, surely I cannot contribute to hope in the world. And if I am not committed to hope in the world, surely I cannot contribute to hope inside my own life.

If enough of us support each other in this cause, we can reinforce it in our common life. Hope means struggle, keeping on, and refusing to give up. But still, in this single moment of fatigue and listlessness, I could more easily give up than do anything else.

Enflame my desire to survive, God. Disturb me.

Nurture my instinct to embrace life. Do not leave me alone in the death of selfish contentment.

Wrestle with me, I pray you, God.

How do I find peace amid the wars inside and outside myself? Invariably I seek a perspective of life that bursts loose from the limitations and imprisoning ghettos of simply my own experience.

For example, I struggle with all the energy that I can summon to extend my thinking and feeling beyond stultifying categories that would strangle promise and hope, incarnate cynicism and despair, and deny the mystery and reality of God in ordinary life. I have learned that, in order to achieve necessary and new levels of identity as a human being, I must fight against programed existence. So I have to enter streams of consciousness, essentially by means of deeper human experiences and relationships, that shatter rigidities within my own thought and spiritual patterns.

Yes, this can be painful. This is one of its virtues, for it wars against both a self-induced and a socially manipulated tranquilizing. I struggle to survive and grow by reminding myself, in a dozen, a hundred, a thousand ways, that I am a person. This involves me immediately in God's world of people. None of us is really altogether good or bad; all of us are mixtures of these; our lives are intertwined with selfishness and generosity, hard practicality and vision, agony and laughter.

I LONG FOR THE RUNNING OF THIS NEW DAY

But, God, I also have my fears about it.
Yours is the power and
Why can't I?
Take my body and soul
But give me
I have this strong need
Forever and ever
I want
On earth as it is in heaven
Show me
Your will be done
How shall I?
Faith, hope, love, but the greatest of these is
God, here is my hand
I hurt. I'm hungry. I itch. I fear. I struggle.
    I hope. I thirst
God, you know I'm a short-distance runner
Yet the course to run is long
You are loving, ready to run with me
Am I running with you, God?